SONORAN
STRANGE

Logan Phillips

DAVID —
QUE VIVA EL STRANGE

4/2014
TUC

First print edition: January 2015
ISBN 978-0-9910742-5-9
West End Press | P.O. Box 27334 | Albuquerque, NM 87125
For book information, see our website at www.westendpress.org

Cover photograph: Logan Phillips
Cover illustration: Spring Winders
Typography and design: Lila Sanchez
Photographs courtesy of: Logan Phillips (33-34, 66, 112); Kira Olsen (65); Emiliano Leonardi (85); and Nayla Altamirano (111)

S O N O R A N

S T R A N G E

¿No es un dolor
que este artículo de primera necesidad
(respeto a nuestra situación)
no lo podemos fabricar

teniendo, como tenemos,
materiales con abundancia
entre nosotros?

> —*Don Pedro Baptista Pino,*
> *New Mexican Delegate*
> *to the Cortes de Cádiz, 1812*

In our studies of landscape we are very frequently made the victims of either illusion or delusion. The eye or the mind deceives us, and sometimes the two may join forces to our complete confusion. We are not willing to admit different reports of an appearance. The Anglo - Saxon in us insists that there can be only one truth, and everything else must be error. The reality is one thing, the appearance quite another thing; but why are not both of them truthful?

> —*John C. Van Dyke,*
> *"The Desert," 1903.*

The empire is nothing but a zodiac of the mind's phantasms.

> —*Italo Calvino*

No están mudos la tierra ni el tiempo.

> —*Eduardo Galeano*

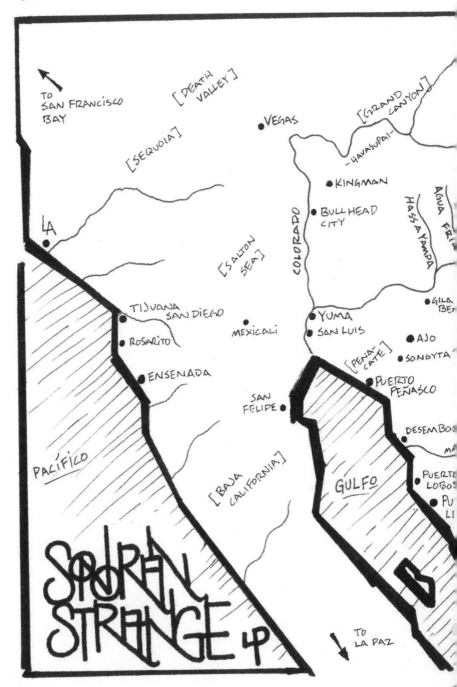

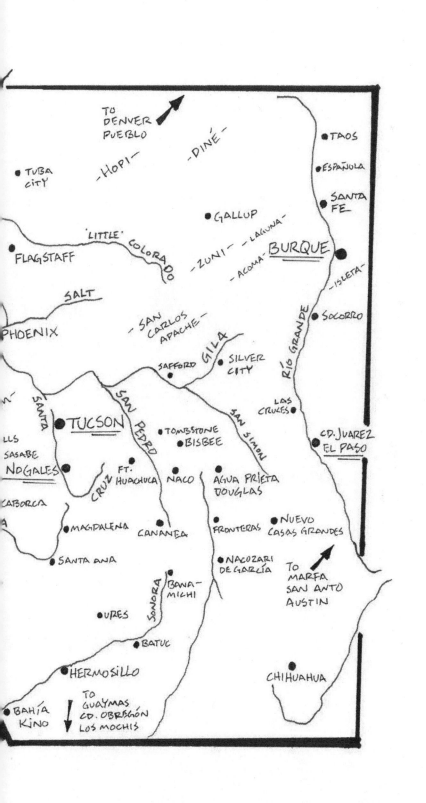

Oposura, Cosari, Jocome

Tesia, Tórim, Nacatóbari

Nacozari, Papigochic, Yécora

Baviácora, Baserac, Tónichi

Nácori, Guévari, Aconchi

Suamca, Cuquiárachi, Dolores

Fronteras, Hac Arituaba,

Cananea, Tubac, Batuc,

Arizonac.

And it is here that the great spine of the continent goes underground.
No Rockies, no Sierra Madre Occidental, but
instead only isolated mountains of pine
rising thousands of feet above the desert floor; sky islands
floating in a sea of desert,
        surrounded by coral of cacti.

        Millennial migratory route for thousands of bird species
        and millions of humans, this is the far northern range
        of the ghost-like Mexican jaguar
        and the parrot-like Elegant Trogon,
            moving between islands of prehistoric tropics.

This is where Aldo Leopold coined the term *conservation*.
This is where hundreds of people are left to die every year,
        lost at sea, an ocean of desert, *naúfragos*.

        From these peaks Anglos conquered the valleys,
        sending military Morse code
        in the reflection of heliograph mirrors.
        From these peaks Anglos reach towards the sky, trying
            to untangle the stars in observatories.

In these wide valleys shipping lines were mapped.
This is the crossroads that gave the railroad tycoons
a flat route for the transcontinental railroad;
                east to west, west to east, cattle and tourism.

                This is the crossroads that gave aboriginal cultures
                a direct route for their transcontinental commerce;
                                south to north, north to south, turquoise and jade.

Esta es la tierra que le dio a México su mina de cobre más grande,
the earth that gave the United States its largest copper mine,
                this is the wealth of empires.

                This was where the Mexican Revolution began
                and Manifest Destiny ended,
                                washing back from California.

Anglo bandits escaped here after raiding in Mexico.
                Apache bandits escaped here after raiding in Mexico.
Mexican narcos stage here before smuggling into Arizona.
                Phoenicians escape here in summer, to second homes.
Tucsonans slide here in winter, on Sonoran ski slopes.

Homeland of the Chiricahua Apache, homeland of the Huachuca agave.
Where the O'odham were born, where the thunder is born;
psychogeographic landscape of myth. Hollow with limestone caverns,
punctured by prospectors. Lost treasure and endangered species.
             Extinct zip codes and boomtowns and the holiest of places.

             Baboquivari and Ramsey.
             Timber and perennial springs. Suppression and crown fires.
             Santa Rita and Catalina. Pinaleños and Peloncillos.
             Tumacacori and El Tigre.

Sky islands float
             like blue mirage,
             under black thunderheads
             and above waves of irradiant
             desert summer.

This is for the endangered languages.
This is for the unnoticed realities.
This is for the lesser-recognized senses.

This is for anyone who has forgotten their mother tongue.
Éste va para cualquier migrante lingüístico,
       refugiado en el verbo.

This is for every mouth that once spoke Mexican
       and now speaks sand just forty miles
       as the vulture flies from where we now stand.

This is for anyone who drinks earth in the end,
       no water for their lost thirst at last.

This is for every cactus ripped out by the roots
       to make room for eighteen holes.
This is for every snowbird
       on their last flight, golfing one last eighteen.
This is for every gila monster
       driving a dropped Cadillac through desert.
This is for every rancher
       resisting the city.
This is for every language teacher
       alive in the tongue-dance of history.

This is for all the cotton
       that was pulled from the irrigation
       and woven into tires for war.

This is for all the copper
       that was pulled from pits and made into bullets
       to kill men fighting in trenches.

This is for all the men fighting and mining in trenches,
      wearing their jobs on their flesh like a skin color.

This is for every youth who remembers.
This is for every elder who imagines.
This is for every chingona.
This is for every fronterizo.

Este poema va para Tucson, su sinfín de sueños,
      su historia presente, su tiempo cíclico,
      sus barrios arrasados, sus estudios étnicos,
      su espanglish, su gringañol.

Este poema va para Tucson,
      y para todos los cabrones
      que aquí viven, y que aquí cantan:

      Arizona, aguanta—el pueblo se levanta.

Sonoran strange hiding in the creosote.
Overhead the stars are spinning a spiral,

sky built of jetstream, laced with
jet trails in angular web.

Sonoran strange slitting
the throat of hundred-year cacti,
pleading for June water
with near-dead tongue,
saltface, sandlung.

Aren't we all
just liquid hiding
behind spines?

Sonoran strange, Maricopa County,
a golf course without lube.

Sonoran strange, Pima County,
6th & Stone may be my bones
but history will never hurt me.

Sonoran strange, everywhere
the obvious has gone into hiding.

Limestone caverns,
        yet to be discovered.
Cochise's bones
        yet to be discovered.
Cabeza de Vaca,
        yet to be discovered.
Lost paradise,
        yet to be discovered.

The true location of the border,
        yet to be discovered.
The next bonanza,
        yet to be discovered.
The extent of this,
        yet to be discovered.

        Sonoran strange, trains filled with tanks.

        Birds building nests of nylon y nopales.
        Packrats building nests of cotton and hair.
        Hummingbirds flying transcontinental.

        Jumping cholla jumping borders,
                sun climbing the fence everyday.
        Tumbleweeds sowing their foreign seed.
        Sycamores strangled with drought.
        Heavy rain hanging on the horizon.

        Saguaros in bloom,
                uprooted by poachers, sold
                on black market of cacti.
        Saguaros in fruit,
                injected by rangers, protected
                with tracking devices.

        Titan missiles growing among saguaro,
                dreaming again of
                an intercontinental blooming.
        Ocotillo forests, subdivisions of hogans.

        Momentary minutemen,
                a patriotism of convenience.

Cowboy governors, trading on myths
    bought from tourist brochures,
    scorpions for breakfast.
Internment camping trips, vacations at gunpoint.

Hubcap heliographs,
    holding dreams of being stars again.
Sunshine and tanning salons.

        The shotguns, itching for trespass.
        The freeway exchanges, noosing into knots.

        The migrations of dust devils.
        The genocide of tumbleweeds.
        The infidelity of founding fathers.
        The tubercular ghettoes.
        The heat combustion of dumpsters.
        The birth of atomic bombs.
        The skin cancer of moonlight.
        The osteoporosis of saguaro skeletons.
        The co-evolution of agave flower and moth.
        The whispers of radio towers.
        The etymology of *OK*.
        The export of mattresses.
        The exploitation of labor.
        The right to work.

    Sonoran strange,
        the cliché cemented in caliche.
    Sonoran strange,
        the chupacabras of scapegoats.

Mangas Coloradas cutting telegraph wires,
Llorona haunting the canals of Scottsdale,
Lupe lining her eyes, rolling on the southside,
shotgun lumberjack lost in a saguaro forest.

A woman kneels at El Tiradito, prays to San Agustín,
        y San Francisco, promises una manda de sangre.
A man who builds cathedrals of mud
        describes working adobe
        as being like kissing his grandmother.
A girl is kidnapped and later found alive
        in a box buried in the desert.

Sonoran strange,
self-storage units, half full,
arroyos carved of stone, half full,
the old neighborhood, half empty,
the aquifer, half empty,
foreclosed boomtowns, ghost towns,
the clock turned off with the electricity.

        Sonoran strange, all the obvious in hiding,
        Cortés weeping over the body of Moctezuma.
        Mexica rituals in front of Schieffelin Hall, Tombstone.
        Silver nuggets and cocaine kilos.

            The Tucson Mountains, lips of an ancient volcano,
                dreaming again of lava breath.

                The Catalinas had a sex change
                    and became cumulus clouds,
                while the thunderheads grew heavy & butch
                    and became the Rincons.

The Chiricauhuas, the Whetstones,
jaguars caught in surveillance.
The Superstitions, the Huachucas,
Jones' Gold, an Arizonan Ophir.

The desert billboards, strung
between neurons, like cities hanging
in the web of freeways.

The state bird
is being flipped
all up and down Interstate 10
as Interstate 10 devours neighborhoods.

Under the terms of Guadalupe Hidalgo,
all Mexicans living in the new United States
were made to cut the treaty
into tiny paper squares
and hold them under their tongues
until they dissolved and the new
reality set in.

This legal precedent is used
to set state immigration policy to this day.

ARIZONA FREEWAY SUNRISE

Interstate 10, just south of the Gila River

Grasses are always dancing in the median, headbangers,
seed sowers, dry spines twisting.Freeway flowers face early decapitation—
guillotine tirewind, lit by skyfire:

here the sun is literally a star,made of beaten copper,
sharp, imperfect. As the star pulls itself up again, the sky
goes streaked, the improbablepattern of yellow-red, vivid.

The radio stations are murmurs in the Spanglish static
The cities hide behind the horizons.The tires break
grass necks.The flowers throw themselves, colorful,
suicidal philanthropists, into the east-bound,
into the west-bound.

Saguaro shadows are spinning sundialson the clock face
of burning sand;
they tick, they spin, they speakuntil they're spoken to,
ripped out,paved over, left in piles, sold.

The rush, the hush, the hiss of wind and
the immutable silence of light.

The piston explosions,the cellphone syllables.

Two realities in the same moment.Two landscapes
that never touch.

Arizona freeway sunrise.A breeze blowing
through barbwire.

JW POWELL DEFINES CAÑÓN FOR ANGLOPHONE READERS

First we shall eliminate the tilde,
that swoop of typography over our *N*—
let us excise the *Ñ* that gives us a sound
behind the average American throat.

Let us approximate with the insertion of the letter *Y.*
Let us remove the spike of the accent from our *O*—
     from *cañón* to *canyon,*
let us continue to travel downstream.
Indeed, let us push onwards toward the meaning of canyon,
let us hear from my journal entries
made in the wilds of the West,
for only in context can a canyon be understood.

First, the general aspect of that country:

     low, arid, hot, and naked, volcanic mountains scattered here and there,
     lone and desolate. During the long months the sun pours its heat
     upon the rocks and sands, untempered
     by clouds above or forest shades beneath.

     Smooth faces of naked rock, some
     composed of marls, disintegrated material,
     through which one walks as in a bed of ashes.

     Low, fleshy plants with bayonets and thorns—
     club-like stems of plants armed with stilettos.
     Many of these plants bear gorgeous flowers.

And secondly, the meaning of the word:

     these canyons
     are alike changeable

in their topographic characteristics—
consider the action of one of these streams.
The river continually deepens its beds;
so that all the streams cut deeper and still deeper,
until their banks are towering cliffs of solid rock.
These deep, narrow gorges are called canyons.

Every river has cut another canyon;
every lateral creek has cut a canyon;
every brook runs in a canyon;
every rill born of a shower
and born again of a shower
and living only during these showers
has cut for itself a canyon.

A million cascade brooks unite to form a thousand torrent creeks;
a thousand torrent creeks unite to form half a hundred rivers
beset with cataracts; half a hundred roaring rivers unite
to form the Colorado, which rolls, a mad, turbid stream,
into the Gulf of California.

All of the scenic features of this canyon land
are on a giant scale, strange and weird.
The streams run at depths almost inaccessible,
lashing the rocks which beset their channels,
rolling in rapids and plunging in falls and
making a wild music which but adds to
the gloom of solitude.

Bold escarpments, scores of hundreds
of miles in length—great geographic steps,
thousands of feet in altitude—a mosaic of many colors,
polished by the drifting sands and glistening in the sunlight.

To wit:

we think of the mountains as forming clouds about their brows,
but the clouds have formed the mountains—the wandering clouds,
the tempest-bearing clouds, the rainbow-decked clouds
carve out canyons and cliffs and mountains.

In the imagination the clouds belong to the sky,
but when they are in the canyon,
the skies come down into the gorges.

It is a land of music, but more:
it is a vast district of country.

JW POWELL MAKES HIS CASE TO THE GENERAL PUBLIC

Indeed, ladies and gentlemen,
the blank spaces on our maps are but insults
to our industrious nature, blank canvases
on which we shall paint *new-found lands.*

I put to you
that this land is ours for the mapping,
that time is ours for the keeping—
neither the scale nor age of this geology
should impede us from acting upon it,

given the crest of our intellect,
the deftness of our reckoning
and the science begun by our fathers;

having now belonged
to the United States for two decades,
various government expeditions
have already penetrated these regions.

CANTO RILLITO (WITH BATS UNDER BRIDGES)

El bisabuelo de tu tatarabuelo es ahora
aquel arroyo que serpentea en la montaña.

Rillito rillín, riote río
Rio-ito más pequeño cada año
Rillito rillín, riote río
Cada año, más arena que agua

Bats get a good day's sleep
while the city rushes in circles.
Bats whose new caves are under the bridges
built to hold the hurry of the city:
overpass caverns.

Do bats dream in sonar, wings pulled tight?
What is the pitch of high noon?
What does a stoplight sound like?
Who are the oldest poblanos of the Old Pueblo?

Rillito rillín, luego cae la noche, radiante.

At dusk, you can watch the shadows flip over themselves
in somersault as the sun sinks its heat
on the heavy mirage of the horizon jagged.

The saguaro sundials stand still.
The sunset stops traffic,
El atardecer arde prendido.

This is when the desert inhales
after holding its breath all day, the moment
the bridges let their cement bones creak
when the skies let their colors leak.

This is when the desert lets its life show,
ghost sand water begins to flow,
life comes out into the night.

Night flowers begin
to bloom, a reflection of stars.

Murciélagos, estos residentes persistentes,
esta gente desértica, voladora, bailadora
dip duck dive feeding through the sunset:

bats, bits
of night
sky broken
off, flirting
with fading daylight,
a living cloud of ink.

¿De qué son los sueños de murciélagos?
¿De bichos deliciosos y voladores?
¿De un Rillito con agua?
¿De las noches sin faroles?

Río-ito, agua mito
aun en agosto.

Rillito we call you río-ito
little river smaller every year,
dimunitivo.

After every year,
Rillito rechiquito.

¿Pero es río pequeño
o es río empequeñicido?
¿Quién traga el Rillito enterito?
What are the bats dreaming about,
as their wings bend in ballet?

Who gets invited to eat at the water table?
Who has lost their water table manners?
Who drinks too much?
Who remembers the Rillito as more than sand?
Who drinks eight glasses a day?
Who putts eighteen holes a day?
Who sprays pesticides every day?
Who drinks too much, leaving only sand?

Flirting with the first dark of night,

     esta gente desértica, voladora, bailadora,

the living night of this desert,
the living desert in this night,
murciélagos sobrevivientes
floreciendo bajo los puentes.

      Murciélagos sobrevivientes
      floreciendo bajo los puentes.

CHIRICAHUAS SOLD A BARREL AT THE GATES

Presidio of Tucson, May 1856

Late sun; sweat
pulled from the pores
by the giant sweat-eating sky.
Slowly drying up
there, spirits and steel.

Under suicide glide of sun, fifty nearly dead
drunk on periphery of presidio. Whiskey
in wounded wood, barrel from back
where whiskey is born, brought on
wagon train to the edge, to the adobe
fortress under changing flags.
Dark liquor & dark lips.

> Leather is a type of skin.
> Barrel tastes like gunmetal,
> like the fingers near the lips.
>
> Sun-hot, glass made with lead,
> oil dancing on the outskirts of water
>
> Whiskey, well-sat in sun, burning
> the gut, held in its skeleton racks;
> the barrel bound in its metal straps.

Camped there along the Santa Cruz,
the Chiricahuas are sold a barrel, sold

a slow powder keg,
a weapon to dull the stories.

Alcohol—a way of negotiating,
sign language of fist and grimace.

Alcohol held in the gut
as the horizon grows dim.

LUPE, IN LINE OUTSIDE THE CLUB

In that skirt you'd never recognize her,
her eyes not upturned but eye-lined.
She's got the tiara, wearing
the full crown to the club would be too much.
Hair straightened and halfway down the brown skin of her back,
ear lobes hooped, you probably wouldn't recognize her.

Without the hábito, you probably wouldn't recognize her,
stars on her fingers rather than in the fabric, puro bling.
Her heels, and the way she seems to float on them
over the cold broken sidewalk; her friends
flocking like little angels, foundation on their cherub faces;
with them you might not recognize her.

Her face seems familiar though—maybe you're friends on the internet.
Maybe she was at the club that one night when your homie
got all drunk and started crying and shit and was looking for someone
to talk to, rather than texting his ex-girl more apologies.

Doing something besides saving your ass, you might not recognize her.
Just out to have a good time, you might not recognize her.
You might not recognize her, rolling her eyes

at all the problems created tonight
that are going to need fixing tomorrow.

DAVE GRINDMAN SPEAKS SHOTGUN TO THE SAGUARO

You damn thing.
Ain't got nothin to say that my gun can't say better.

What am I doing here; this deserts a goddamn wasteland,
nothin good outta it; get my sawed-off.

Boy, this is the gunpowder show,
I hold thunder behind a fingernail.

      Tell me I won't do it. A six pack says I will.

Goddamn million of you. Always talkin.
      Got somethin thicker to say to you.

        Got a trigger in my finger; hottern hell out here.
        Time to teach you what fallin feels like—

• • •

    Well look a that.
    I'm a bonafide cactus lumberjack,
        ain't I? Tell you, feels good
            to watch yer green flesh fly,
                white of yer ribs. I am this man.

Teach you what fallin

                  feels like; few more shells now,
    I got all
        afternoon; this deserts
         a wasteland.
    Set to speak

          so y'all can hear me,

      you damn thing—

PUERTO PEÑASCO

The pelicans dive.
The shrimpers dredge.
The airplanes fly to Los Angeles.

Mountains float on surface of horizon.
Palm trees shoot, slow-motion
        chlorophyll fireworks.

Ghosts of extinct sharks
        tickle the toes of the swimmers.

Little birds run on the sand.
Vacation homes empty like litter.
Satellite dishes searching the sky—
        atheists in prayer.

Tonight the shrimping boats are stars that fell but didn't drown,
instead they found a buoyancy on the salty swirl of gulf.

Out there, hanging, unsure of the difference between sky & sea.
Out there, desconociendo la barda entre la arena y el agua.

INDIGENOUS INSURGENTS STORM OBSERVATORY, REAPPROPRIATE TELESCOPE'S GIANT MIRROR

Arizona Republic, page A1

PHOENIX – Calling it the *heliograph sent to rewrite the treaties,*
today the ransom was set at 40 million acres and a buffalo
herd of 40 million, to be transferred immediately.

Otherwise the gargantuan solar laser will be precision-focused
to send a beam of searing light from Cerro Tololo at Kitt Peak
into the cooling pumps of the Palo Verde nuclear power plant.

Reached at Los Alamos, nuclear experts remained adamant
that the attack, which would surely cause meltdown, was not their fault.
We didn't know the uranium mines would cause cancer on the reservations!

In the ransom note, the insurgents admitted
as to where they stole the technology used
to weaponize the thirteen-foot astrological mirror.

What? You motherfuckers think we weren't paying attention
when you taught us to make solar ovens in your elementary schools,
the letter asked, adding, *Hotdogs? Think bigger, bitches!*

In the valley below,
the panic was general
and the traffic gridlocked.

Asked for comment, one driver remarked
Give em back the goddamn desert
if they want it so bad! We never meant no harm,

concluding,
they're a-fixin to pop us like ants
under a magnifying glass!

LLORONA, AS TOLD ON THE TELEPHONE
(BY MOTHERS IN SCOTTSDALE)

You know how Cindy and I walk the canal in the morning, well
today I think I *saw that woman again,* you know, the one
I was telling you about, that I saw a couple months ago,
homeless and crazy and skinny and Mexican?

Well today *I saw her again,* I know
she's some kind of dangerous—I heard she's in and out of jail,
homeless, probably *illegal.* She looks like a meth addict, huffing paint.
You know I think she drowned her children in the canal—

yes, *that* kind of dangerous. She should be locked up.
I think she lives down there, talking to herself in Spanish all the time.
It's like she can't leave the spot where she *drowned her children—*
if I were you I wouldn't let Tommy walk home from school

along the canal, I think she lives down there, I heard her talking—
you know, where I walk with Cindy in the mornings.
If I were you I'd pick Tommy up from school,
I'm telling you, I've been seeing her for months.

Sonoran strange,
telephone pole fingers—
wire tangled in the knuckles.

Giant powerpoles on the rez
built to look like kachinas
woven in traditional Hopi blankets,
the same way the high-voltage lines
stitch themselves into the dawn, on
the loom of landscape
and the myth of progress.

Cellphone towers built to look like saguaros.
Saguaros grown to look like cellphone towers.

        Stripmines torn to build tract housing,
        closed mine, foreclosed housing,
        strip malls, strip joints,
        empty subdivisions
        and fifty in a drophouse.

    Quivira, Eldorado,
    Cibola, the Seven Cities of Copper.

    Cananea, built by the mine.
    Cananea, eaten by the mine.

    Labor, built by the mine.
    Labor, broken by the mine.

Manifest destiny:
extraction economy,
exploitation economy,
extinction economy,

bull market, bear market, expand or die,
cannibalism as business model, ditat deus.

> Uranium & bombs
> & silver & mercury
> & astronomy & cotton
> & Pluto & real estate
> & gold & asbestos
> & subdivisions & military contracts
> & cattle & legend
> & citrus & vitriol
> & missiles & timber
> & assault rifles & sunshine
> & prisons & postcards
> & resorts & scenic overlooks.

> On Día de los Muertos, aviators
> visit the airplane graveyard.

> There they drink bacanora
> and make war noises with their mouths,
> while the sharp-toothed smiles
> of the airplanes stare ever forward.

> Mothballs and marigolds, there with
> employees of the bomb factory
> and those that follow orders to drop them

> —they toast to the extinction economy.

Didn't anyone think to send the saguaros to boarding school
      where they could learn to look more like elm,
    to lie more like cherry trees?

Who decided to stop teaching the saguaros
      about where they came from, to stop teaching
      about the ironwood, about the palo verde
      about the nurse plants that shaded them
      during the first years of Sonoran sun,
      allowing them to survive their first years in this soil?

Who banned the ethnic studies of cacti,
      demanding that they learn only the waters of the Potomac
      and not to question why the Santa Cruz runs dry,
     why the Gila runs dry; what good is the Potomac
    if the Colorado runs dry?

Who looked at our spines and only understood blood,
     only saw aggression instead of understanding
    this place and why spines are needed sometimes?

              Who notices genocide of saguaro?
              Who notices buffelgrass and subdivisions?
              Who holds any idea of history, psychobiology?

              Who misquoted the clouds into right angles?
              Did they quote the coyotes in the case against the ranchers?
              Didn't anyone tell the wildfires about anti-smoking laws?

              Where did Padre Kino retire to?
              Where did Coronado retire to?

Is the governor listening?
Is there someone here from the city council?
From the school board?
Is anyone here from the FBI?
Can you please raise your hand if you are here under cover?

Is this being recorded?
Is anyone sending a text message right now?

Is there someone here that was born in the area?
Is this any good?
Is anyone with me?

OZYMANDIAS FOR MAYOR OF PHOENIX

Transcript of remarks at press conference, 2/14/2012

Good afternoon, all, thank you for coming—
today is an important day in our great state of Arizona.

Today I am formally declaring my campaign
to be the next commander of our prosperous city.

It is clear from my time as Director of the Salt River Project
that I am a sculptor, whose epic works in cement

have pushed the desert farther from our city, while celebrating
our desert's unique ecosystem and knack for attracting tourism.

Ladies and gentlemen, my fellow Arizonans,

I believe in the evaporative cooler. I believe in water
misters on restaurant patios, in *efficient* crops like cotton and citrus.

I believe in twelve lanes for Interstate 10, I believe in Freeway Loops
101, 202, 303 *and* 404. I believe through parking lots *we can do more.*

May I forever be known as Ozymandias, Mayor of Mayors!
May future generations marvel at what we did

here in mighty Phoenix! May those people despair in knowing
that only what *we* have built here will last for all time!

PHOENIX, SOMETIME AFTER MAYOR OZYMANDIAS

Nothing beside remains. Round the decay
Of that colossal wreck, boundless and bare
The lone and level sands stretch far away.

EDWARD ABBEY'S CAMPAIGN OF TERROR

Ed Abbey tags Unisource Energy Building
H - A - Y - D - U - K - E O - N - E

Ed Abbey tags Bisbee Copper Queen Hotel
G - O - L - I - A - T - H

Ed Abbey tags air-conditioned trailer of Predator Drone pilot
C - O - W - A - R - D

Ed Abbey tags Titan Missile Museum
F - I - R - E O - N T - H - E
M - O - U - N - T - A - I - N

Ed Abbey tags any number of malls
B - U - Y N - O - W

Ed Abbey tags bathroom mirror, Maricopa County Juvenile Court

L - O - N - E - S - O - M - E
C - O - W - B - O - Y

Ed Abbey keys unmarked Border Patrol S.U.V.
___ ___ __ _____ _____ __

Ed Abbey dine-&-dashes at El Tovar, Grand Canyon.

Ed Abbey inner-tubes Central Arizona Project.

Ed Abbey refuses to check his email.

Ed Abbey says some racist bullshit.

Ed Abbey speaks chainsaw to billboard.

Ed Abbey spins in his grave,
        an electric turbine,
        a renewable resource.

CHIRICAHUAS GIVEN THE TERMS OF SURRENDER

Dragoon Mountains, October 1872

Dawn the color of a coal held on the tongue.
An awakening of horses. Flies about the mouth
and nose after whiskey vespers, interment of fire ring.

Morning of the meeting near Slavin Gulch,
council held on rocks
in a stronghold of granite.
The collision of concepts and poetics.
Fingers slide across rifle throats,
communication through an intermediary.

Gunsights—a technique for seeing eye to eye,
ay to ay yay, a swollen tongue, a loss of consonants;
not a loss of territory but of a reality, a language.

Terms of surrender—if Geronimo then Crook,
if Bascom then Camp Grant, if massacre then massacre,
if territory then genocide—a simplification of terms,
a weaponization of language.

Treaty written in script of barbwire:
word equation of Western logic,
rectangle of civilized men,
geometry of European progress, division.

The first day of hereafter:
as long as the stone shall last,
this peace will remain unbroken.

        Litany of canyon wren,
        daggered teeth of acacia,
        rocks the color of dawn.

Surrender—a giving-over into the hands
of another—a manner of consenting to oblivion?

TOURIST IN HARMONIOUS COLOR AFFECT

Arizona Highways Magazine, 1936

Exquisite workmanship!
Harmonious color effects!
Yet always weird,
inhuman and grotesque.

Fantastic headdresses!
Gorgeous costumes!
Sun colors!
Bright feathers!
Beating Tom-Toms!
Haunting chants!
Fantastic serpents!
Thrilling!

Different and exquisite
are these remarkable dances.

IN CIUDAD JUÁREZ THEY SAY THE NIGHT IS A THIEF

but it was not the night that stole you,
night wrapped warm around forehead and under your arms,
it was men whose shadows have climbed into their hearts.

Jalisco verde, a childhood in seabreeze
spent naming clouds: *libélula, golondrina*. Then older,
to the north, to work. But it was not the night that stole you.

The face of Mamá argued with itself, tears over smile.
Papá, moustache black and words: *bye, cuídate mucho,
there are men who have swallowed their own shadows.*

El Norte means hope and hope is a four-letter word
spoken between bleeding fingers, between shifts. Then
the night stole the day and you waited

for the bus, thick footsteps in sand behind you.
Men whistled and called. Then their fingers tore,
their shadows swollen inside you.

It is said the longest night births the most beautiful sun.
You, far away in wind. May it never be said that
it was the night that stole you, for it was men
who still walk wearing badges but casting no shadows.

ARIZONA CONSTELLATIONS

State Highway 86, somewhere outside Ajo

Once thrown from speeding windows—

now sun-scorched,
now monsoon-rinsed,
littered labels now wordless.

> Some shattered back into stars,
> green glint & brown shine & clear shard, they
> watch sky spin by, burn of days, twirl of night.

> Some unbroken, hold together,
> drink rain and hold wet inside themselves—
> a trick they learned from the saguaro.

> Saguaro, who have cradled rain
> since before they were themselves.

>> So bottles become terrariums,
>> abandoned glass holding planets—
>> all planets but containers of water.

>> Inside, thimble thunderheads:
>> rain again, condense again,
>> water beads, water runs,
>> wind blows across hollow—
>> a lonely thunder.

>>> Ants come here to pray.
>>> Ants carry waterdrops
>>> larger than themselves
>>> down into earth,

where they stack them
in their caverns like boulders,
in their storerooms like fruit,
in their cathedrals like sacrament.

Meanwhile, car windows unnotice

civilization of insects,
climate of planets,
constellations shattered
across desert floor.

LLORONA, SQUATTER IN FORECLOSED BACKYARD

From the canal side,
jumping the backyard wall is easy,
        cinderblock is mostly hollow.
Usually, though, she just opens the gate.

The bank changed the padlock,
        took the house, gave it to no one.
Llorona changed the padlock back,
        gave the house to herself.

Picking locks is easy,
        a question of time with nowhere to go.
Usually, though, she sleeps on the back porch.

Through the dust-colored windows
her eyes trace all that she left behind
        the morning the bank came.

                Sometimes, though, a smile in the eyes,
                she sees wisps of her children
                        still playing in there, still here—

                All these houses were built to look the same,
                        is this the same house?

                        Are the children still
                                out playing by the canal?

Sonoran strange,
>> just who do you think we are?

Nos toman por hijos de puta,
>> nos(otros), hijos de la frontera.

The people assumed to be Mexicans
>> who aren't always Mexicans.
The people assumed to be white
>> and might not be white people.

The Mexicans who don't speak Spanish
>> and the Mormons who do.
The Mexicans with their papers, que se sienten superiores.
>> United Statesians without passports, not worth the trouble.

>>>> The Chicano speaking Spanish on cellphone
>>>>> in his Border Patrol uniform
>>>>> at the freeway checkpoint.

>>>> The gringo foreign exchange student
>>>>> who feels más mexicano que la chingada
>>>>> y que ha aprendido bien que no
>>>>> hay nada más mexicano que la chingada.

>>>> The native teenager riding the Yo-Yo in Sells,
>>>>> Tohono O'odham Nation, Rodeo and Fair;
>>>>> feeling herself spin around the horizon
>>>>> and the horizon spinning inside her.

>>>> The high school kids playing with their kids
>>>>> after school at their mom's house.

Los chiapanecos chambeando en el norte.
Snowbirds sunning in the south.

Sonoran strange, such as it is,
one man's norte is another man's sur.
La puta de uno es madre de otro.

>Sonorizona.
>La rumerosa, la maquila,
>Barrio Heavy, Barrio Libre.

>>The border used to be main street, Nogales,
>>>now it's concrete poured into pipe dreams.

>>First they built the wall of rusted military metal,
>>>old landing strips used in the first Gulf War.

>>>(Then torches spoke acetylene angles,
>>>>bundles passed through kilo-shaped holes.)

>>>*(Show me a fifty-foot wall,*
>>>>*and I'll show you a fifty-one foot ladder.)*

>>Then they built a *virtual fence* of military contracts.
>>>Motion-sensing cameras caught raindrops
>>>migrating from the monsoon, sin permiso.

>>>The border wall, now a series of columns,
>>>>a set of ideas, made to feel permanent.

Sonorizona.
Las prostis, los pochos
y las puestas del sol.

The nomadic truckers waiting for free trade,
        folding pesos into paper airplanes,
        watching them fly through La Mariposa;

the drivers less free than the cargo they carry.

Sonoran strange, all things being unequal,
        we're more ourselves on the edges,
        wearing our hearts on the outskirts
        and holding the hollow inside us.

                The miners, out of work,
                        digging international tunnels,
                        tunnels with air conditioning and telephones.

                In Nogales they say a drug tunnel
                        is busted every other day.

                In Nogales they say one day the centro
                        will collapse into all these empty veins.

So much more to us
        than seen on our surface,

sonoran strange,
        just who do we think we are?

SALSOLA TRAGUS

Tierra-tragante, disturbante, compadre of dust.
Circle seed-spitter, tumbling thistle.
Salsola, que solo sale, sal sol que le quiere ver.

Stow-away in grain crop seeds.
Unsettling settler, wagon wheel automaton.

Gluttonous globalizer, coat-tailer of developer,
carpetbag colonializer, hugger of highway shoulder.
Plaque of bulldozer teeth, pubes of pavement.

Allergen, argonaut,
continental heir, thorned air,
wind witch, chamizo volador,
terreno violador, conquistador.

Eurasian mar-andante, noxious navigator,
Bering Strait shooter, Russian random thistle,
stock trope exploding across freeway grill.

> Wagon trains, steamboats, railroads,
> interstates, bus lines, sky harbors.

> Telegraph, heliograph, telephone,
> radio, broadband, satellite.

> Salsola tragus, drifting along,
> *I know when night has gone*
> *that a new world's born at dawn.*

WAYS OF TELLING A STORY: BRIGHT ANGEL

I.

This archeological dig
explores a site that was active
800–1250 A.D.
and later abandoned,
possibly due to famine,
mismanagement of resources,
or war. It is unknown
what became of the inhabitants.

II.

This village
was continuously occupied by humans
for twice as long as the United States
has been a country.
After this time,
the peoples changed
and formed other villages.
Their descendants continue
to live in the area to this day.

WAYS OF TELLING A STORY: FORT HUACHUCA

I.

Fort Huachuca was founded in 1877
to secure the Mexican border
and to fight the Apache Wars.

From 1913 to 1933, the fort was home to the 10th Calvary,
the *Buffalo Soldiers,* one of the first peacetime all-African American regiments
in the regular U.S. Army. Already having earned a distinguished record
during the Indian Wars, these honored soldiers also fought
in the Spanish-American War, the Philippine-American War,
the Mexican Expedition, the Battle of Ambos Nogales
and the Battle of Bear Valley.

Today Fort Huachuca is home
to the US Army Military Intelligence Center
and the 111th Military Intelligence Brigade;

the installation is an important contributor
to the economic well-being of Cochise County.

II.

Fort Huachuca was founded in 1877
to protect the Gadsden Purchase
and finish the indigenous genocide of North America.

After Arizonan statehood, the fort was home to the *Buffalo Soldiers,*
descendants of African slaves, sent by commanders
to invade Cuba, the Philippines, and Mexico (twice).
In 1918, following orders from Capt. *Blondy* Ryder,
the soldiers fought and captured the last band of indigenous insurgents,
a group of Yaqui who were fighting the Mexican government
for the establishment of an autonomous state.

Today Fort Huachuca is home
to the interrogators of Abu Ghraib
and practice flights of Predator drone;

the installation is an important contributor
to the economic well-being of Cochise County.

PUERTO LOBOS

Lost to clocks, swaying in tide.
Fish by night, sleep by day.

Ghosts of sharks
circle the panga.

Population of wind,
promised electricity.

Shipwrecked on the coast, here where the land runs out;
the continent is also an island, there's no way off of it.
Some fishermen have shipwrecked inside themselves,
run aground, only here because they are nowhere else.

When the cellphone tower finally reached this far
the voices were unsure what to say but spoke anyway,
in the evanescent manner of humans.

Local government: an empty elementary school
and a police station of broken windows.

The walls aren't as much walls
as whatever they were
before being walls.

Old fishing nets strung as fences
after they became tired of killing.
Round bones of sea turtles stacked outside the door.
Hermit crabs trying on the glass of coke bottles.

Desert cliffs falling into sea.
Volcanic rocks reaching up through the waves.

Ocotillos holding up white plastic bags—
surrender, litter
of fishbones and birdbones
and other skeletons in between.

None of the ghosts in Lobos are people,
those have left by now.

Lobos, last of the land,
between sky and sea, the beach,

      the sand, tiny rocks,
      children of boulders
      waiting to grow up
      into mountains.

TOURISTS PONDER DISASTER
(OF TOURISTS, WHO FELL FROM SKY)

MID-AIR COLLISION OVER GRAND CANYON—
DEADLIEST AIRLINE CRASH IN NATION'S HISTORY

I.

Sit back, relax and we'll try give you a good loo—
and down there folks you'll see the Grand Cany—

Planewrecked on skyshore,
closer than they intended, strewn across

the sights they set out to see, they and
their craft shattered—to mirror shards,
sprinkled over a rock named after a temple.

II.

Make sure your life jacket is securely fas—
look closely folks, they wrecked just about here
you may still see bits of mirro—

Adrift on surface current,
holding binoculars to eyes, looking

at strands of mirage, into shards of mirror.
If they look closely enough they will find no one
looking back—from a rock named after a temple.

III.

Collision of conveniences,
the awkward feeling of mortality—

thus the choice (through binoculars):
these tourists choose to feel superior to *those* tourists
who died doing *this* same touring.

ARIZONAN INSURGENTS GIVE TACTICAL ADVICE TO AFGHANI INSURGENTS
or Mangas Coloradas Gives Tactical Advice to the Taliban

They like their wars cold at first.
Our first word of English was *proxy* also.

We know that they once sold you guns under the table,
and we know that the land you claim hasn't been yours all that long.

It was the same for us.

Our place was this to them, too.
Middle East, Far West, the same:

California, named after the caliphs and myths they expected to find here,
mesquite trees named after the mosques they liked to burn there.

Afghanistan, Arizona, anglicizations
of words from tongues they do not speak.

They test drone airplanes there.
They tested nuclear bombs here.

They sent their immigrants to fight us, led by assimilationist officers,
        under the illusion that to die for them would be to be accepted by them.
        We called those soldiers *buffalo.*
They send their poor to fight you, led by ROTC officers,
        under the illusion that PTSD would help them pay for college.
        They call you *sand niggers.*

We know war like you know war.

Afraid to take on the Spanish Empire and the Mexicans,
      they bought the livestock we stole from the Spanish ranchers
      and their arms dealers gave us Remington rifles.
      More cows, more rifles, more Spanish settlements burned.
It was convenient for them.

Afraid to take on the Soviet Empire
      their agents took you and trained you
      and their arms dealers gave you rocket launchers.
      More money, more guns, more Soviet tanks burned.
It was convenient for them,

we also learned the word *opportunism*.

Later, they tried to occupy the land
like the Spanish and Soviets before them.
They called us *enemy* and we
turned their guns back on them,
and fought like they had taught us too.

And still later, on this land,
on that land, they learned
very slowly the word *negotiate*

but still couldn't quite get *memory*.

LLORONA STANDING NEAR CANAL AT MIDNIGHT

A moon mirage amid night shadow,
she takes small steps in sand
along cement bank.

                    The sound of sirens at night
                    the orange of city sky
                    and whisper of jets, distant traffic.

Staring at the slow water of
the Arizona Canal, she looks for them here

along the cement channel,
in the paved-over indigenous design.

Dark hoodie over layers of clothes.
Thin skin, thin bones.

Gallon jugs yellowed & brittle from sun,
liquor mixed from the bottles abandoned by backyard parties,
bottles holding bodies of drowned scorpions,

                    millipedes, mice, small snakes—
                    she collects the drowned,
                    sings to them.

Sonoran strange,
how long till the water runs out?

Sonoran strange,
have you hidden the monsoon
between your ears, water
pouring from your face?

Monsoons in centenarian fight
to make it down to the aquifer;

have you frozen the monsoon
into the icecubes in your drink?

Drought dodger,
sand irrigator,
irrational instigator,

artesian artisan,
oasis schemer,
optimist for profit,

canal digger,
developer,
line drawer,

civilizer, glutton, goner.
Ditat deus.

Never wanted to hide in the rain shadows?
Never wanted to face the dry music?
Well don't dare speak of tightening the sunbelt

in Cibola, the Seven Cities of Aquifer,
the irrigated never-neverland.

Conquistador archeologists
stealing fossil water, not-for-long land.

Water in our eyes and humid sighs,
such as we are we shit into drinking water
because it is convenient.

And this poem is only as nihilistic
as Arizona was overly optimistic.

Depredation,
privatization,
privation,
pordioseros,
ditat deus.

What do the monsoons taste like
after their waters have been aged
a thousand years in a sand aquifer, reposados?
Can you tell me what sand tastes
like on the rocks? What it looks
like, sand in the toilet bowl, what it looks
like, sand pouring from the tap in the kitchen,
what it sounds like, sand streaming from the carwash?
What does it look like, a man
stooping to suck from the sprinklers in Papago Park?
What does it look like, sand shooting from the sprinklers,
drowning the golf course in its dry breath?

Water management plan:
we'll inject all of the empty water bottles
back into the earth, to prop up our cities
before they sink into empty aquifers.

Western states holding the Colorado River
hostage, nothing flowing into Mexico.

Evaporation tanks flooding Hayduke canyons,
Central Arizona Project delaying the inevitable.

Hetch Hetchy, Glenn Canyon, Echo Park.

Water dancing in drops,
spilling from the sky,
the sky an inverse aquifer.

Paloverde trees on drip systems.
The elderly on drip systems.
Everyone holding a drop of hope.

Phoenix needs its fix, fall-
into-a-panic drought, a
pandemic, paranoid of the
obvious—oblivious by choice.

We'll irrigate our way outta
    this we'll irradiate
    our way outta this
    we'll entertain
    our
    way
    outta
    this,
    fatal
    this.

        Everyone's skeleton is a pueblo
        some have seen more rain than others.

        The only reconquista
        that really matters
        is the coming victory
        of dust and coyotes.

        We'll see this, you and I:
        the day thirst returns to the desert.

LUPE, REAL TALK (OVER RASPADOS)

Mostly I don't give a shit what they say about me.
It's not like I need their permission.
Really, they just like that I'm popular,
it's been that way from the beginning.
What do they call that? Swag by association?

John Paul acts like he knows me—
we just met! I never promised *him* anything.

Not like any of them are paying my bills anyway.
I have all these sisters coming to me all the time
with that man-drama, I don't need any of that myself.

> Did you see that house they built me in el D.F.?
> Shit's crazy, girl.
>
> Everybody always showing up on their knees, though.
> All bloody. I mean I never asked them to do that, I swear
> sometimes que a la banda le gusta sufrir, straight up.

I should've bought stock in a candle company.
Mi prima, Maria, was talking about opening up
an abarrotes ahí por El Altar, selling veladoras,
pero le dije que eso se llama algo como nepotismo
and besides, sería mal visto—de muy mal gusto.

> Closest thing I ever had to a man was that dude
> Juan. We weren't together, but people
> make assumptions, you know? Saw us together
> and him with the roses and just assumed.

I was hanging with la raza esa all the time then.
But again, what? Bishop whats-his-name
hears about it, starts acting like he knows me,
like I'm one of their crew and I'm like *yo,*

since when did I ever agree that I'd just stand there
smiling and keeping my mouth shut?
That ain't me.

Damn girl I told you
I was gonna get all worked up
over this. You finished?
What'd you get, anyway?
Beso de Ángel?
Word.

CYLINDROPUNTIA FULGIDA

Fortress of wren, holder of nest,
needled crib, godfather to egg
—aflame in dawnlight, the wrencall.

Jumping cholla, la brincadora,
la viajera, la vela de coyote, to:ta hanam
—alight in a lightness of being, borderless.

Drinker of sand, halo of bones,
chain-hanger, cylindropuntia fulgida
—a bit of sun, earth-fallen, taken aroot.

Spear-haired trickster, dagger-eyed freeloader,
angelic bonsai, skeleton of desert coral
—all juxtapositions endemic to desert.

Thick-skinned traveler,
mohawked hitch-hiker
—along for the ride, stuck on my boot.

FURTHER EXCERPTS FROM RANSOM LETTER

Sun, sun, you came for the sun,
sun you come & sun you go, so
much of a good thing:

> we're focusing it here,
> and will echo it across the state.

Heliographs. Your army used the sun
to send Morse code from mirrors on mountaintops
after we learned to cut telegraph wires,
tying in cowhide to cover the break.

Do you think we weren't paying attention?

We'll send Phoenix back to ashes—
dust to dust and all that
we learned in your churches.

> Behold this solar-powered decolonization!
> Behold this Pine Ridge of saguaro!
> Behold this Pueblo Revolt with lasers!

Your canals are based on Hohokam technology
—when has the Salt River Project ever paid royalties?
Intellectual property rights are another one-sided treaty.

First your churches and prisons,
next your schools and liquor stores
then the casinos and mines and powerplants—
gambling and linguistic extinction and satellite dishes,

have you noticed the shape of your progress?

So Palo Verde goes first, Hoover Dam next—
if the meltdown and flood don't get you,
then your own heat bubble will:

we'll do to the air conditioners
what your bullets did to buffalo.

Yes, we're holding the Hohokam Expressway hostage.

The name *anasazi* will someday be yours, too—
disappeared ones. You, we, all of this—

Why?
>   Because I'm from here
>   and spent my first years
>   in a house built on caliche.

Why?
>   My father's back bent over the shovel,
>   planting agave in the front yard,
>   where car bones later came to rest.

Why?
>   Because this tongue
>   is what I make of it
>   y hablar es creer.

Why?
>   Because my diapers
>   are buried in unmarked graves
>   outside Tombstone.

Why?
>   Because I learned
>   of where I'm from
>   while I was the farthest away.

Why? Because we're the fastest-growing state in the union.
Why? Because we have the second-highest poverty rate in the union.
Why? Because we fund education less than any state in the union.
Why? Because state legislators are big fish in an evaporating pond.
Why? Because statistics will blind you if you stare at them long enough.

Why? Because it's not too late,
>   it's just too much lately.
Why? Because it's always too much,
>   it's just never enough really.

¿Por qué? Porque este pueblo trae un corazón mexicano,
      una cara mestiza y una cartera gringa.
¿Por qué? Porque nadie recuerda bien los tratados,
      los poemas hechas ley, los huesos hechos de adobe.
¿Por qué? Porque la cultura es una capa, nada más,
      pintada sobre la faz de la tierra, una y otra vez.
¿Por qué? Pues por qué no, hay que buscar un por qué por ahí.

        ¡Que viva la Baja Arizona!
        ¡Que viva la Otra Arizona!
        ¡Que viva la Sonora Libre!

        ¿Que viva? Qué va… ya vive,
          ¿A poco no la ves?

LLORONA SPEAKING AT PAYPHONE

— Yes hello, what is your emergency?
— Hay un cuerpo en el canal.

— Hold on just a second, ok—
      do you speak English, ma'am?
— Lo saqué yo a la orilla y lo amarré ahí.
— A body in the canal?

— Lo salvé como siempre salvo lo ahogado
      en las albercas abandonadas por ustedes.
— Can you tell me where the body is? …dónde?
— Los sigo buscando siempre,
      pero este cuerpo no es de ellos,
      lo encontré buscándolos.

— I need you to tell me where …dónde están?
— ¿Dónde no, mujer? Ser madre es ver
      tus hijos en todas partes para siempre.
— Could you please speak slower? …I'm also a mother—
— Ser madre es parir el propio corazón de una
      y vivir para verlo andar por todas partes siempre.

— If you can just hold on, the police will be there
      in a few moments, you can show them where you found it—
— No van a querer ver nada de lo que les puedo enseñar yo.
      Este cuerpo lo encontré ahí flotando y solo les estoy diciendo
      porque este cuerpo también tiene madre, siempre.

— The police will be able to help, I just need you to stay on the line.
— Contaminaron el canal con furia, me quitaron todo…
— Drownings sometimes happen, this wasn't your fault.
— Mis hijos…

— I understand this is difficult,
      being a mother is like giving birth to your own heart.
      Where are you? Are your children there with you now?

LLORONA STANDING NEAR CANAL AT DAWN

A shadow haloed in sunglare,

unseen by eyes that cannot see her,
that choose to look away. Ignore her,
joggers & headphones.

She adds her salt to the canal deadwater.
Unsilent grief. River of salt. Valley of sun.

      Canals become saline,
      their waters pull salt from the land.

         Palm trees, pigeons,
         hawks on powerpoles,
         mourning doves.

PUERTO LIBERTAD

Pueblo
of heavy-winded sunset sandblast,
smokestacks, heavymetals & endless desert.

El beso de arena y agua
—voice breaking, macho student
says how much he loves it, how angry
he is at the word *ugly.*

In the trailer-classroom, desks in a circle—
> *here we are holding poetry as a worker holds a tool.*
> *We are building community through self-expression,*
> *opening the gates to the pueblo inside our chests, fíjate que*
> *tus locuras son bien parecidas a las mías, carnal—*

At the powerplant, no scrubbers
since it's an *unpopulated area.*

> Burning chapopote, bunker fuel.
> The wind incessant, blowing
> out to sea this year.

> The fishermen, fishing.

Somebody said the poor laugh more,
dance more. Idealization,

sure, but also algo de verdad
at least in Libertad, donde

el pueblo no es pobre
y no hay de otra.

SAGUARO FLATTENS DAVE GRINDMAN, SPEAKS:

By the time your body is found,
your shooting arm, taken by the coyotes,
will be stripped to bone while they laugh.
The rest of you I will hold under me, still.

Taken by the desert, your shooting arm
will be the only part of you to escape.
The rest of you I will crush with my body.
Funny how we managed to coincide so well.

The only part of you to escape
will be long gone by the time they find you,
they will think it funny how I squashed you.
I will be ready to relent to their chainsaws,

you will have turned black and we will be inseparable.
Striped into my ribs, punctured with my spines,
I will be ready to show them what the desert can do
by the time they find you.

Inseparable, they will carry us back into Phoenix together,
under the cover of night, under the cover of tarp
so that others on the freeway will not see you,
will not see what the desert can do.

Eventually, they will all know, and
I teach this lesson to your people gladly.

SONORAN STRANGE: BARBWIRE

Sonoran strange,
there are ghosts hanging in the barbwire.

> All the dead ranchers, pondering slaughter weight.
> All the dead bulls, creosote dancing behind the eyes.
> All the dead trees, souls hanging in smoke above the fire.
> All the dead lungers, dust and miasma.
> All the dead vigilantes, buried back east.
> All the dead governors, bolo ties and sweetheart deals.
> All the dead voters, poll taxes and literacy tests.
> All the dead soil, sacrificed to cotton.
> All the dead migrants, bones defying statistics.
> All the dead Chinese, spines of iron track and skin of scapegoat.
> All the dead laborers, bones buried in cement of Hoover Dam.
> All the dead saguaro, toothpicks in the teeth of bulldozers.
> All the dead Hohokam, wandering wide fields of agave.
> All the dead Yaquis, wrapped in henequen, sovereign in sand and sky.
> All the drowned kachinas, singing among refrigerators at the bottom
> of Powell Reservoir.
> All the ghosts, hanging in the barbwire.

¿Y nosotros? ¿A poco no somos?
> Que también sonambulamos,
> cargados con deberes, quehaceres.
¿A poco no morimos y nacemos cada día?

Sonoran strange,
> los muertos también viven
> y los vivos también se mueren.

And when I say dead what I mean to say is alive,
> when I say past what I mean to say is what's to come,
> when I say you what I mean to say is me
> when I say me what I mean to say is we.

Geronimo, escaping into the canyons.
Snowbirds, escaping into the pitstops.
Cochise, escaping into the stronghold.
Easterners, escaping into the Wild West.
Developers, escaping into retirement
Phoenicians, escaping into the AC.
Investors, escaping into the 5th Amendment.
Ghosts, escaping into spook.
Poets, escaping into the words.
All of us, escaping to somewhere else, if not into this.

Y nosotros,
¿Quiénes somos, olvidando el pasado?
¿Quiénes somos, tragando el mito de un paraíso?
¿Quiénes somos, bailando brevemente?

      ¿Y qué es esta vida sino un baile de luces?

            Sonoran strange,
            souls and the rocks,
            the spines and clocks.

            Souls and the rocks,
            the spines and clocks.

NAMING: TOMBSTONE

Greaterville, Harshaw, Silver Bell

Galeyville, Dragoon, Pearce

Duquesne, Washington Camp, Courtland

Evansville, Helvetia, Gleeson

Dos Cabezas, Turquoise, Middlemarch

Paradise, Russelville, Black Diamond

Mammoth, Oracle, Total Wreck,

Winkelman, Hilltop, Globe,

Tombstone.

NOTES ON THE POEMS

NAMING: ARIZONA · 9

The name "Arizona" can be traced back to being used by the Spanish for an area of silver mining near Nogales starting in the 1730's, but from there, the origins get murky. Given that many of the Spanish were of Basque origin, it could be that "Arizona" is from the Basque *aritz ona* or "the good oak tree." However, it is most likely derived from the O'odham phrase *'Al şonag* or "place of the small spring," which would explain in the inclusion of the final *c*. Names are layers of paint we lay upon the land.

Officer, James E. *Hispanic Arizona, 1536–1856.* (Tucson: University of Arizona Press, 1987).

West, Robert C. *Sonora: Its Geographical Personality.* (Austin: University of Texas Press, 1993).

SONORAN STRANGE: SKY ISLANDS · 11

The sky island mountain ranges are the defining feature of a geographical area that spans the modern states of southeastern Arizona, southwestern New Mexico, northeastern Sonora and northwestern Chihuahua. Between the ranges are vast areas of high desert grassland and mesquite scrub which mark the transition between the Sonoran and Chihuahuan deserts. Unable to cross the wide desert valleys, unique species of plants and animals evolved here, becoming endemic to their particular ranges. For this reason, what is today the U.S.-Mexico borderlands is a vast stronghold of biodiversity, even surpassing the diversity and richness of the human cultures that inhabit and pass through the area.

SONORAN STRANGE: CUK ŞON · 14

The modern name of *Tucson* has its roots in the indigenous O'odham name *Cuk Şon,* or *Black Base,* a reference to the city's location at the base of a distinctive volcanic mountain range. The site has been continuously occupied for more than 4,000 years, branching out from its genesis point in the fertile agricultural fields planted along the lush desert river that ran through the area. Today that place is known as the base of "A" Mountain near the Santa Cruz River; the long-cultivated fields were later used as a landfill from 1953 to 1960, after the river had been pumped mostly dry. Despite this and the many attempts at erasure—"urban renewal" projects such as the Tucson

Convention Center—the city still holds one of the longest unbroken human legacies in contemporary Arizona.

For more on Arizona's great cotton boom and bust during World War I—200,000 acres in 1920—see Sheridan's *Arizona*.

Meeks, Eric V. *Border Citizens: The Making of Indians, Mexicans and Anglos in Arizona*. (Austin: University of Texas Press, 1997).

Otero, Lydia R. *La Calle: Spatial Conflicts and Urban Renewal in a Southwest City*. (Tucson: University of Arizona Press, 2010).

Sheridan, Thomas E. *Arizona: A History*. (Tucson: University of Arizona Press, 1995).

———. *Los Tucsonenses: The Mexican Community in Tucson, 1854–1941*. (Tucson: University of Arizona Press, 1986.)

SONORAN STRANGE: GILA · 16

The Gila River is the central river of the Sonoran Strange, draining almost the entire territory. After the United States' invasion and occupation of Mexico, from 1846-48, the treaty of Guadalupe-Hidalgo used the river's course to designate the new boundary between the two countries. The border wasn't moved to its present location until the Gadsden Purchase was signed five years later in 1853. Now mostly unnoticed and dry except at its headwaters, the Gila River's flow was once perennial and sufficient for navigation from its mouth near Yuma to the modern Arizona-New Mexico border. Now, arid Maricopa County in the Gila River Watershed has more golf courses per capita than any other county in the United States.

Álvaro Núñez Cabeza de Vaca was a Spanish conquistador who, after shipwrecking during an attempted invasion of the Florida peninsula in 1527, was one out of only four survivors from a force of 300-plus who walked roughly 6,000 miles over eight haunting years from present-day Florida to north-central Mexico. On their long sojourn "into the sunset," they traveled in concert with many indigenous tribes who revered them as healers. The four men from the Old World were the first to see much of what would eventually be colonized as the southern United States and northern Mexico. The party included an African slave, Esteban, who was later instrumental in guiding Spanish explorations of the territory and beginning a long African legacy in the Southwest United States and coastal Mexico.

El Tiradito, also known as the Wishing Shrine, has been an important locus of Tucson culture since soon after it was built in the 1870's. Though it has shifted position three times, it has mostly survived gentrification and is located on what is now Main Avenue, just south of the Tucson Convention Center. The

TCC, not coincidently, stands atop what was once La Calle, one of the city's earliest barrios and a vibrant home to generations of Tucsonans of Mexican descent. La Calle was razed in the late 1960's in an "urban renewal" effort led by Tucson's business and political elite—most of whom were Anglo. Before being destroyed, La Calle had suffered from years of municipal neglect but was still "the most densely populated 80 acres in Arizona," according to historian Lydia Otero. The fight for El Tiradito's inclusion on the National Register of Historic Places in 1971 was a critical moment for the preservation of what was left of La Calle, which was slated to be destroyed by the freeway. Thanks to tireless efforts of community members including Alva Torres and many others, folded wish-poems still fill the crevices of the pock-marked adobe wall behind the flickering candles of El Tiradito, in what is now known as Barrio Viejo or Barrio Histórico.

Eliazar Herreras graduated from the University of Arizona in 1921 and worked as Tucson's building inspector from 1930 to 1953. His skill with adobe was immortalized by the newspaper *El Tucsonense* who quoted him as saying "it's like kissing your grandmother. I was born in an adobe house, I smelled it, I saw adobe made from the beginning—it is just something I know." Herreras was instrumental in preserving jewels of Tucson's architectural heritage such as El Tiradito, Mission San Xavier del Bac and the cathedral dedicated to Tucson's patron saint, San Agustín.

The girl's name was June Robles. In 1934, she was the six-year-old granddaughter of some of Tucson's wealthiest citizens. June was kidnapped for ransom and later found alive in an iron box in the desert east of the city where she had been buried for nineteen days.

Leo Banks, "The Girl Locked in the Desert Cage: Tucson approaches the 70th anniversary of one of its most notorious criminal cases—one that remains a mystery to this day," *Tucson Weekly*, November 27, 2003.

Cabana de Vaca, Álvar Núñez. Covey, Cyclone. *Cabeza de Vaca's Adventures in the Unknown Interior of America*. (Albuquerque: University of New Mexico Press, 1983).

Dennis R. Bell, et al. "Barrio Historico Tucson: Urban Rehabilitation Option, Fall 1971/72." College of Architecture, University of Arizona, 1972.

Otero, Lydia R. *La Calle*.

Sheridan, Thomas E. *Los Tucsonenses*.

Sonnichsen, C.L. *Tucson: The Life and Times of an American City*. (Norman: University of Oklahoma Press, 1982).

ARIZONA FREEWAY SUNRISE · 21

For more, see the eastern horizon at first light from any point along the transporta-
tion arteries of Arizona. This poem was first published in the chapbook *Where Do
Airplanes Build Their Nests?* in 2007.

JW POWELL DEFINES FOR ANGLOPHONE READERS · 22

Much of this is a found poem, quoted directly from John Wesley Powell's *Exploration
of the Colorado River and its Canyons,* first published in 1895 and considered a classic
of Southwestern Literature. Major JW Powell, one-armed U.S. Civil War veteran and
then head of the U.S. Geological Survey, was the first recorded European to make an
extensive exploratory expedition in the canyons of the Colorado River watershed, in-
cluding the Grand Canyon, in 1869.

Powell, J.W. *The Exploration of the Colorado River and Its Canyons.*
(New York: Dover, 1895, 1961).

JW POWELL MAKES HIS CASE TO THE GENERAL PUBLIC · 25

"Whatever in creation exists without my knowledge exists without my consent."

—The judge, in *Blood Meridian*

Frederick Turner gives far and away the best examination of the Western need for
constant expansion and quantitative definition, which gave rise to the idea of
"Manifest Destiny."

McCarthy, Cormac. *Blood Meridian or the Evening Redness
in the West.* (New York: Random House, 1985).

Turner, Frederick. *Beyond Geography: The Western Spirit Against the
Wilderness.* (New Brunswick: Rutgers University Press, 1980, 1994).

CANTO RILLITO (WITH BATS UNDER BRIDGES) · 26

"The great grandfather of your great-great grandfather is now that arroyo
that snakes in the mountain."

—Eduardo Galeano

Commissioned by the Rillito River Project for their 2009 performance art event Bat
Night, this poem was first performed in the riverbed under the Campbell Avenue
bridge in Tucson.

The Mexican free-tailed bat *(Tadarida brasiliensis)* migrates between what is now the western United States and central Mexico, but their populations are in wide decline. The Rillito once flowed year-round in the northern Tucson basin, draining the Catalina and Rincon mountains. In our time it floods only occasionally after large monsoons and has been transformed from its original wide, shallow course to a deep channel that quickly moves water away from the area. This has been the shared fate of many Arizonan rivers, most notably among them the Santa Cruz and the Salt.

This poem previously appeared in *Ground\Water: The Art, Design, and Science of a Dry River*, Confluencenter for Creative Inquiry, The University of Arizona Press, 2012.

Galeano, Eduardo. *Espejos: Una Historia Casi Universal.*
(México DF: Siglo XXI, 2008).

Phillips, Steven J. and Wentworth Comus, Patricia, eds.
A Natural History of the Sonoran Desert. (Tucson: Arizona-Sonora
Desert Museum Press/University of California Press, 1999).

Sheridan, Thomas E. *Los Tucsonenses.*

CHIRICAHUAS SOLD A BARREL AT THE GATES · 29

"Horse blood or any blood a tremor ran that perilous architecture and the ponies stood rigid and quivering in the reddened sunrise and the desert under them hummed like a snare drum."

—Cormac McCarthy

This poem is a rendering of a scene imagined by McCarthy in his seminal novel *Blood Meridian.* The Western conquest of Las Américas becomes clearer when understanding it as a war waged not only with steel and gunpowder, but also using economic, biological and linguistic weapons.

The Chiricahuas were a tribe of Athabaskan-speaking Apaches present as a distinctive group in Arizona since the mid-1500s, or perhaps much earlier. The word *Apache* was coined by the Spanish, probably versioned from the Zuñi word *'a paču* meaning "enemy." The Apaches called themselves *tinneh, dine, nnēē, tinde,* or *inde,* words from multiple dialects with varied spellings that all translate as "Man," "Human Beings," or "People." That Western history knows them by their enemies' label testifies to the context of war and conquest in which the cultures first encountered each other.

McCarthy, Cormac. *Blood Meridian or the Evening Redness in the West.*

Sweeny, Edwin R. *From Cochise to Geronimo: The Chiricahua Apaches, 1874–1886.*
(Norman: University of Oklahoma Press, 2010).

LUPE IN LINE OUTSIDE THE CLUB · 30

See the sidewalks along Congress Street in downtown Tucson on any weekend night, c. 2008.

DAVE GRINDMAN SPEAKS SHOTGUN TO THE SAGUARO · 31

Saguaro, the largest cactus found north of the present U.S.-Mexico border, are particularly slow-growing in their natural habitat. They can take 30 years to grow from a seedling to 2' tall, and 65 years to reach 8', at which time they generally begin to flower. A fully mature saguaro with many arms can be 250 years old or older.

Now finding themselves in a state with lax gun laws and wide deserts, Arizonan cacti have a long history of being used for target practice.

Tony Davis, "Ironwood Forest Killers of Saguaros Strike Again"
Arizona Daily Star, December 30, 2011.

Phillips, Steven J. and Wentworth Comus, Patricia, eds.
A Natural History of the Sonoran Desert.

PUERTO PEÑASCO · 35

Also known as Rocky Point, legend has it that this one-time sleepy fishing village on the coast of the Gulf of California began its transformation into a playground for Arizonans sometime around Prohibition in the 1920's, when the first thirsty gringos began to arrive for the Mexican beer and beaches. Nearly all of the opulent hotels and seaside mansions remain empty for most of the year, awaiting vacationers. The economic downturn of 2008 and reports of drug-related violence in Northern Mexico were a plague to the local economy, which is based on constant growth and the service industries. Overbuilding and speculation have left many coastal structures half-built.

INDIGENOUS INSURGENTS STORM OBSERVATORY · 36

Scientists and astronomers in the United States have long been interested in using the southwestern part of the country for studying the stars. Observatories dot several peaks of the sky island ranges, among them Mount Graham and Kitt Peak. Construction of these peaks has always come at odds with other uses and indigenous belief systems involving the mountains, leading to lengthy court battles concerning the conservation of endangered animal species and the spiritual rights of indigenous peoples.

The Palo Verde Nuclear Generating Station is the only civilian nuclear installation in Arizona and became the largest power plant in the United States by net generation when it came online in the mid 1980's. Located near Tonopah, the reactors are about 45 miles west of downtown Phoenix—one of the most rapidly expanding urban areas in the country.

LLORONA AS TOLD ON THE TELEPHONE · 37

The Arizona Canal of central Maricopa County was built from 1883-85 to divert water from the Salt River into agricultural fields in the northern valley. It is nearly fifty miles long, making up a large part of the Salt River Project's canal system, which totals 131 miles. Today the canal runs through some of the most affluent communities in the state. As with all canals in Phoenix, the banks of the Arizona provides a popular route for runners, walkers and bicyclists. During the winter months, the mild temperatures also attract transient populations to cities and their waterways across the southwest.

SONORAN STRANGE: CIBOLA · 38

Every one of the infamous "Five C's" of the twentieth century Arizonan economy was based on labor and the extraction of natural resources: cotton, citrus, cattle, climate (tourism and development) and most of all, copper. Bisbee's Copper Queen Mine (in operation from 1880-1975) was one of the most important in the U.S., while just over the present-day border, the open pit in Cananea is still Mexico's largest copper mine.

Bisbee was the largest mining district in the Arizona Territory to operate as a "white man's camp," an exclusionary agreement which operated through what a local reporter at the time characterized as "unanimous unwritten consent." This racist rule was primarily aimed at two groups: Chinese, who were barred being in the district after sunset, and Mexicans, who were not allowed to work underground, where the highest-paid mining jobs were. For more on this, see Benton-Cohen's incisive *Borderline Americans*.

Another pillar of Arizona's economy is the U.S. military, which goes unmentioned in the Five C's either because its name begins with the wrong letter or because reliance on federal defense spending goes against the state's self-image as a rough-and-tumble, independent frontier. Regardless, the modern versions of both Tucson and Phoenix were founded as military outposts, by the Spanish at Tucson and by the U.S. Army at Camp McDowell at Phoenix. Today, vast stretches of the Sonoran Desert are dedicated to training for war. Raytheon Missile Systems is the largest employer in Southern Arizona. Freeport-McMoRan Copper & Gold—current owner of the Copper Queen Mine—is also in the top five.

Carter, Bill. *Boom, Bust, Boom: A Story About Copper, the Metal that Runs the World.* (Tucson: Schaffner Press, 2012).

Benton-Cohen, Katherine. *Borderline Americans: Racial Division and Labor War in the Arizona Borderlands.* (Cambridge: Harvard University Press, 2009).

Sheridan, Thomas E. *Arizona.*

Tucson Regional Economic Opportunities, "Largest Employers." Accessed 15 January 2012. http://treoaz.org/Data-Center-Largest-Employers.aspx

SONORAN STRANGE: CARLISLE · 40

The children of indigenous tribes living in what is now Arizona began to be sent by Anglo authorities to boarding schools such as the Carlisle Indian School in Pennsylvania in the last decades of the nineteenth century. It is likely that not a single one went willingly. The Indian School in Phoenix was open for nearly a century, closing finally in 1990. These schools were part of the federal government's policies aiming to assimilate the nation's native peoples, a campaign that amounted to an attempt at cultural extermination—bringing "civilization" once and for all to the "barbarous tribes" of North America.

The battle to protect cultural memory and present equal representations of native and Chicano histories in school curricula has been waged by community groups and educators for over half a century, beginning in earnest with the walk-outs at Tucson High School in the late 1960's. It took until the close of the century before a program specifically addressing Chicano and Mexican-American perspectives was instituted in the Tucson Unified School District (TUSD).

Only a decade later, these ethnic studies classes came under attack by Republican members of the state government in Phoenix. After a speech by renowned Chicana labor organizer Dolores Huerta at Tucson High in 2008, numerous bills were introduced in the state legislature targeting TUSD, eventually passing after repeated defeats and leading to the classes being banned in early 2011. The program, which was open to students of all ethnicities and satisfied core curriculum requirements for graduation, continues to have strong community support in Tucson.

Sheridan, Thomas E. *Los Tucsonenses.*

OZYMANDIAS FOR MAYOR OF PHOENIX · 42

I met a traveller from an antique land
Who said: "Two vast and trunkless legs of stone
Stand in the desert. Near them on the sand,
Half sunk, a shattered visage lies, whose frown
And wrinkled lip and sneer of cold command
Tell that its sculptor well those passions read
Which yet survive, stamped on these lifeless things,
The hand that mocked them and the heart that fed.
And on the pedestal these words appear:
'My name is Ozymandias, King of Kings:
Look on my works, ye mighty, and despair!'
Nothing beside remains. Round the decay
Of that colossal wreck, boundless and bare,
The lone and level sands stretch far away."

"Ozymandias," Percy Bysshe Shelly. 1818.

PHOENIX, SOMETIME AFTER MAYOR OZYMANDIAS · 43

For more on the ironies of water policy in the western United States, see Marc Reisner's indispensible *Cadillac Desert*.

Reiner, Marc. *Cadillac Desert: The American West and Its Disappearing Water*. (New York: Penguin Books, 1986).

EDWARD ABBEY'S CAMPAIGN OF TERROR · 44

Author of *The Monkey Wrench Gang* and *Desert Solitaire: A Season in the Wilderness*, the controversial writer left an indelible mark on the Southwestern psyche by celebrating popular militant environmentalism.

Abbey, Edward. *The Monkey Wrench Gang*. (New York: Avon Books, 1975).

CHIRICAHUAS GIVEN THE TERMS OF SURRENDER · 46

The four Chiricahua Apache bands (Chihenne, Bedonkohe, Chokonen and Nednhi) were among the last groups of native people to surrender their autonomy to the recently-arrived U.S. government. Among their infamous warriors were the feared— now celebrated—figures of Mangas Coloradas, Juh, Chatto, Naiche, Cochise and Geronimo. This poem describes the morning of a pivotal meeting between Cochise and General Oliver O. Howard, at which the Chokonen leader made peace with the United States after waging a twelve-year war against its military. An expert historian on this topic is Sweeney, and Jacoby's *Shadows At Dawn* offers critical context.

> Jacoby, Karl. *Shadows at Dawn: An Apache Massacre and the Violence of History.* (New York: Penguin Books, 2008).

> Sweeny, Edwin R. *Cochise: Chiricahua Apache Chief.* (Norman: University of Oklahoma Press, 1991).

TOURIST IN HARMONIOUS COLOR AFFECT · 47

This found poem is taken verbatim from a 1936 edition of *Arizona Highways,* the state's monthly tourism-advocacy magazine, as quoted in Sheridan's *Arizona.*

> Sheridan, Thomas E. *Arizona.*

IN CIUDAD JUÁREZ THEY SAY THE NIGHT IS A THIEF · 48

The exponential growth over the last half century of border cities such as Juárez, Nogales and Tijuana can be traced generally to the opening of trade between the U.S. and Mexico, and specifically to the phenomenon of maquiladoras. After the 1994 North American Free Trade Agreement (NAFTA), the opportunity for work provided by these manufacturing centers has been a magnetic force for impoverished people throughout Mexico; the maquilas employ tens of thousands of people, many of them women and girls. Since the early 1990's, an estimated 5,000 femicides have been committed by mostly unknown assailants in and around Juárez. It is widely known that the police ignore these crimes and are likely complicit in them. Many of the women raped and murdered in Juárez worked assembling goods for international corporations based in the U.S. and abroad.

This poem first appeared in the chapbook *This Line Drawn Across Footprints,* 2007.

ARIZONA CONSTELLATIONS · 49

A glass bottle has been broken somewhere on the desert floor every weekend night for more than a century.

Arizona was consistently ranked as one of the fastest-growing states in the nation in the 1990's and early 2000's. Following the economic crash of 2008, Arizona suddenly had one of the highest residential foreclosure rates of any state; thousands were evicted from their homes.

> Ohlemacher, Stephen. Vitu, Teya. "Arizona Ends Nevada's 19-year Reign as Fastest-growing State," *Tucson Citizen,* December 21, 2006.

> Arizona Indicators. "Arizona has the 2nd Highest Foreclosure Rate for 2011 Q1." Morrison Institute for Public Policy, Arizona State University. Accessed 09 February 2012. http://arizonaindicators.org/article /arizona-has-2nd-highest-foreclosure-rate-2011-q1

SONORAN STRANGE: AMBOS NOGALES · 52

For Paco Velez.

If interested in the significance of *la chingada* in Mexican vernacular and culture, see Octavio Paz's essay *Sons of La Malinche,* or check the many definitions and uses in the reference book *El Chingonario.*

Former Governor Janet Napolitano railed against the idea of building a wall along the border when the issue was under debate in 2005. The "51-foot ladder" line is quoted from her remarks to the Associated Press at the time.

The Mariposa Port of Entry in Nogales is one of the largest land ports in the United States, where countless tons of fresh produce and other goods covered by NAFTA are imported into the country. NAFTA, signed into law in 1994 by President Bill Clinton, is widely considered to have devastated the rural Mexican economy, forcing millions of campesinos to look elsewhere for work—such as in the United States. Many of these people come from indigenous communities and may not have the basic documents required to gain legal entry—let alone the money required. In the end, hunger usually trumps formality and these people attempt to cross through the dangerous desert east of Nogales near Sásabe. Hundreds of human remains are recovered from this corridor every year—at least 2,000 people have died trying to cross the deserts of Southern Arizona between 2002 and 2012; many more are probably never found.

On any given day south of La Mariposa, miles of trucks are parked, their drivers waiting for permission to bring themselves and the goods they transport into the U.S.

> Banks, Leo W. "Digging for Dollars: The drug cartels have made Nogales the tunnel capital of the Southwestern border." *Tucson Weekly,* April 7, 2011.

Kimble, Megan. "Holding Pattern: A melon's journey from soil in
Sonora to a Safeway on your street," *Edible Baja Arizona,*
Summer 2013: 44–49. Print.

McCombs, Brady. "Nogales to be 'flagship' Port of Entry."
Arizona Daily Star. April 16, 2009.

———. "Sophisticated tunnel found in Nogales,"
Arizona Daily Star. May 10, 2011.

Paz, Octavio. *The Labyrinth of Solitude.* 1950, 1975.

Preston, Julia. "Homeland Security Cancels 'Virtual Fence'
After $1 Billion Is Spent," *The New York Times.* January 14, 2011.

Various authors. *El Chingonario: Use, Reuso y Abuso del Chingar.*
(México DF: Lectorum, 2010).

SALSOLA TRAGUS · 55

The tumbleweed only propagates in soil that has been disturbed—either by development, erosion, or both. The last lines of the poem are taken from the song *Tumbling Tumbleweeds,* composed in the 1930's by Bob Nolan and made famous by the band The Sons of the Pioneers; it later became the title of a 1935 Gene Autry film. For more on the invasive *salsola tragus* and all other species of Sonoran desert life, a definitive reference is *A Natural History of the Sonoran Desert.*

Phillips, Steven J. and Wentworth Comus, Patricia, eds.
A Natural History of the Sonoran Desert.

WAYS OF TELLING A STORY: BRIGHT ANGEL · 56

The first part of this poem is inspired by the interpretative text on exhibit at the Bright Angel Pueblo site in Grand Canyon, whose tone reflects how native presence has traditionally been described by archeologists across the region. The second part of this poem is another way of telling the same story, a translation.

WAYS OF TELLING A STORY: FORT HUACHUCA · 57

Fort Huachuca is located at the base of the eponymous mountain range in southwestern Cochise County, part of the San Pedro River watershed. Major General Barbara Fast was one of the leaders of interrogation efforts at the Abu Ghraib prison when prisoners were tortured by U.S. troops there in 2004. Unlike lower-level soldiers, she was never charged with any crime and was subsequently appointed as Chief of the U.S. Army Intelligence Center at Fort Huachuca.

Carol Ann Alaimo, "Despite Critics, Huachuca's Leader Focuses on Future," *Arizona Daily Star,* July 31, 2005.

Finley, James P. "Buffalo Soldiers at Ft. Huachuca: The Yaqui Fight in Bear Valley," *Huachuca Illustrated,* Volume 2, 1996.

Leckie, William H. *The Buffalo Soldiers: A Narrative of the Negro Cavalry in the West.* (Norman: University of Oklahoma Press, 1967).

Smith, Cornelius C. Jr.. *Fort Huachuca: The Story of a Frontier Post.* Fort Huachuca, Arizona, 1978.

PUERTO LOBOS · 59

There are families of stones
under the ground.
As the young stones grow
they rise slowly like moons.
When they reach the surface
they are old and holy
and when they break open
they give off a rich odor,
each blooming once in the light
after centuries of waiting.

From "Desert" by Richard Shelton. *Selected Poems, 1969–1981.* (Pittsburgh: University of Pittsburgh Press, 1982).

TOURISTS PONDER DISASTER · 61

On Saturday, June 30, 1956, at 10:30 a.m. PST, two passenger airplanes collided over the Grand Canyon. Each pilot had been attempting to give his passengers, tourists, a better view of the scenery. 128 were killed. Today the remote site of the crash is frequently pointed out to sightseers on commercial rafting trips through the canyon.

The evidence for a connection in the European imagination between Arabs of the Middle East and the indigenous people of Las Américas runs deep. An in-depth exploration of the connection between the Crusades and la Conquista is made by Turner in *Beyond Geography.*

Arms trade between merchants in the young United States and the fierce Apache, who in turn used the guns in raids on the Hispanic residents of the Rio Grande Valley, is mentioned in a variety of historical documents, among them Baptista Pino's report on New Mexico for the Spanish Cortes de Cádiz in 1812 and even alluded to in Article XI of the Guadalupe Hidalgo treaty itself. Though there is still no definitive study on the frontier gun trade, Weber contextualizes it well in his *Myth and the History of the Hispanic Southwest,* and it is addressed at length in Jacoby's *Shadows at Dawn.*

The United States' substantial material and logistical support of mujahedeen fighters resisting the Soviet occupation of Afghanistan during the 1980's is also well-documented; it is even the subject of the 2007 Hollywood film, *Charlie Wilson's War.* That some of these weapons and expertise were later turned on U.S. troops fighting in Afghanistan from 2001-2013 is an unpleasant twist, but it certainly shouldn't surprise us, given Afghani traditions of insurgency and resistance to colonialism.

Baptista Pino, Don Pedro. Bustamante, Adrian, Simmons, Marc, trans. *The Exposition on the Province of New Mexico, 1812.* (Santa Fe and Albuquerque: El Rancho de las Golondrinas/ University of New Mexico Press, 1995).

Jacoby, Karl. *Shadows at Dawn.*

Turner, Frederick. *Beyond Geography.*

Weber, David J. *Myth and the History of the Hispanic Southwest, Essays.* (Albuquerque: University of New Mexico Press, 1988).

LLORONA STANDING NEAR CANAL AT MIDNIGHT · 67

The canal systems of the Salt River Valley were first created by the Hohokam people, who were irrigating their fields in the neighboring Gila Valley before the beginning of the Christian era in Europe. In total they dug around 200 miles of canals in the Salt River Valley, the largest of which were forty feet wide and thirteen feet deep, with a perfectly calibrated drop of eight feet per mile. The canals were dug without the aid of animals and sustained an agricultural system that allowed the Hohokam culture to thrive in the area uninterrupted for over 1,000 years with a population of as many as 400,000 people. As Reisner points out, the Valley wouldn't reach this level of population again until the 1920's.

There are many theories as to why the culture dissolved around A.D. 1400. Some point to decreased availability of water due to climate change, or perhaps salt buildup in soils due to over-irrigation. Others believe that European diseases such as measles and smallpox may have arrived before the Europeans themselves did, transmitted ahead of the conquistadores by indigenous travelers along millennial trading routes and decimating the indigenous population here as elsewhere in Las Américas.

Reisner, Marc. *Cadillac Desert.*
Wagoner, Jay J. *Early Arizona: Prehistory to Civil War.*
(Tucson: University of Arizona Press, 1975).

SONORAN STRANGE: SAN PEDRO · 68

"Without more water, we are all going to perish."
—Former Arizona Congressman John Rhodes (as quoted in Reisner, 260)

In the Sonoran Desert, there are five seasons: "wet summer" or monsoon (early July to mid-September), autumn (October and November), winter (December to mid-February), spring (mid-February to April) and "dry summer" or foresummer (May and June). The word *monsoon* is derived from the Arabic word for "season," and generally denotes a wind that changes direction seasonally. Plant and animal species living in this desert have adapted to make the most of the brief, violent storms that can sometimes bring huge amounts of water in a matter of minutes. These floods also create chaos in desert cities, when runoff from parking lots enters streets, underpasses, and channelized urban washes. Every year cars are swept away in the torrents, frequently with their stubborn drivers still inside them.

Ditat deus, the state motto of Arizona, is a Latin phrase translated as "god enriches."

As deserts go, the Sonoran is considered incredibly lush, filled with a wide variety of plant and animal life. In the wide river valleys, the water table sat very close to the surface thanks to millions of years of rainfall accumulated drop by drop. Around the time that Anglo farmers were first beginning to irrigate the old Hohokam fields in the Salt River Valley to feed the soldiers stationed at Fort McDowell, it was possible to dig just a few feet and hit water; in some places liquid literally sprang to the surface in artesian wells.

By the 1960's, some wells in the area were dug as deep as 2,000 feet and still didn't hit potable water. All of the state's principal industries require huge amounts of water to be pumped out of the ground far faster than the seasonal rains can replace it.

The San Pedro is one of the last perennial free-flowing rivers in what is now the southwestern United States. The river made headlines in 2005 when, for the first time in more than 75 years of quantitative record keeping, no water ran in its channel at a measuring station northeast of present-day Sierra Vista. The San Pedro has been at the center of lengthy legal battles, pitting environmental groups against developers and the U.S. Army. Environmentalists contend that Fort Huachuca's water use and ever-expanding housing developments are contributing factors to the decline of the river, which began to be protected in earnest with the establishment of the San Pedro Riparian National Conservation Area in 1988.

Long a corridor for migrations, the San Pedro Valley has the most significant concentration of Paleo-Indian (Clovis) sites, dating back 12,000 years, than anywhere else in North America. While here, the Paleo-Indian peoples hunted mammoth and avoided saber-toothed cats. The San Pedro provided an easy northward route for conquistadores Cabeza de Vaca and Coronado. Padre Kino, Anglo mountain men, and the Mormon Battalion also passed through here. Today, the river hosts millions of migrating birds every year—more than 250 species—constituting two-thirds of the avian diversity in the United States.

"Conserving The San Pedro River Valley's Wealth of Human History."
Archeology Southwest [Tucson], n.d. Web. 12 June 2014.

Tony Davis, "San Pedro River is Running Dry," *Arizona Daily Star,*
July 20, 2005.

Reisner, Marc. *Cadillac Desert.*

Phillips, Steven J. and Wentworth Comus, Patricia, eds.
A Natural History of the Sonoran Desert.

"Places We Protect: San Pedro River, Arizona."
Nature Conservancy, N.p., n.d. Web. June 12, 2014

LUPE, REAL TALK · 72

The raspado is the Mexican antidote to desert heat. Raspados come in many flavors with a variety of ingredients, all of which are more elaborate than those found in the raspado's cousin, shaved ice.

La Virgen de Guadalupe is widely seen to be the Christianization of the goddess Tonantzin, revered by the Nahua people of Central Mexico. The key moment in this process was the apparition of La Virgen to Juan Diego Cuauhtlatoatzin at Tepeyac in 1531. There are innumerable sources that discuss this event, the best of which help place the apparitions seen by Diego in the context of the spiritual war being waged against his people by the Spanish during their first decades on the continent. That La Virgen de Guadalupe was proclaimed patron saint of Latin America in 1910 and Diego canonized in 2002 point to the power indigenous figures continued to have on the Catholic Church.

The modern Basilica of Our Lady of Guadalupe was built in México D.F. in 1976 and is an incredibly important pilgrimage site, visited by over two million people every year. Pope John Paul II first visited the site in 1979.

CYLINDROPUNTIA FULGIDA · 74

This poem was originally written as a commission for Saguaro National Park's BioBlitz biodiversity festival in fall 2011, the literary component of which was organized by poet Eric Magrane. The poem was first published in the online poetry journal *Spiral Orb*, "an experiment in permaculture poetics," edited by Magrane, and also appears in the anthology *A Literary Field Guide to the Sonoran Desert,* University of Arizona Press.

> Phillips, Steven J. and Wentworth Comus, Patricia, eds.
> *A Natural History of the Sonoran Desert.*

FURTHER EXCERPTS FROM THE RANSOM LETTER · 75

See notes for the poem "Llorona Standing Near Canal at Dawn."

SONORAN STRANGE: DRAGOONS · 77

The statistics cited here vary slightly year by year, but not by much.

Baja Arizona refers to the on-again-off-again movement to break off southern Arizona into a new state, whose territory would be comprised of the area acquired by the United States in the Gadsden Purchase of 1853: from the current U.S.-Mexico border on the south to the Gila River on the north. The idea dances in the imaginations of liberal Tucsonans, long at odds with their more conservative counterparts in the current state capital of Phoenix.

The Dragoon Mountains are a sky island range near Tombstone in the San Pedro Valley. The mountains are dotted with beautiful pale pink granite boulders and hold storied sites such Cochise Stronghold and Texas Canyon. Interstate 10 bisects the range just east of Willcox, Arizona.

> Rhonda Bodfield and Andrea Kelly, "Could Baja Arizona Be
> 51st State in US?" *Arizona Daily Star,* February 24, 2011.

In Arizona, drowning is the number one cause of death of children aged one to four. Between the years 2000 and 2013, 108 children died in swimming pools, canals, and other water sources in the City of Phoenix alone. It is indeed an ironic tragedy that this happens in a city surrounded on all sides by desert.

Even in a modern Arizona, there are hospital emergency rooms and social service centers where only English is spoken, in contrast to New Mexico, where government services are bilingual. This contrast dates back to before statehood, when linguistic and cultural arguments were used to justify the opposition to a federal bill that would have admitted the two territories to the Union as one state. In a referendum, New Mexico voted in favor of the measure, while Arizona did not. Congratulating Arizona's dissent, one South Carolina senator characterized the vote as the "cry of a pure blooded white community against the domination of a mixed breed" (Benton-Cohen, 200).

Arizonan politicians have a long tradition of making provocative claims about the level of danger faced by local citizens, usually in a bid to score federal resources. In 2010, two Republican politicians focused on the level of drug-fueled violence in Arizona. On NBC's *Meet the Press,* Senator John McCain called Phoenix the "number two kidnapping capital of the world," while Governor Jan Brewer, on the campaign trail, claimed that "law enforcement agencies have found bodies in the desert either buried or just lying out there that have been beheaded." The evidence supporting these assertions is questionable or nonexistent, and Brewer later admitted to the Associated Press that she "misspoke." While both comments can be dismissed as fear-mongering for political gain, it is important to note that murderous lawlessness has for more than a century been part of Arizona's self-image.

Benton-Cohen, Katherine. *Borderline Americans.*

Children's Safety Zone. "Water Related Incidents Reports 2000–2013 for Maricopa & Pinal Counties," Children's Safety Zone. Accessed 05 June 2014. http://childrensafetyzone.com/go/pdfs/2000_2013_Incidents.pdf

Molly Smith and Stephanie Russo, "Body Found in Canal in Central Phoenix," *The Arizona Republic,* September 15, 2010.

LLORONA STANDING NEAR CANAL AT DAWN · 80

The first ancient Hohokam canal to be cleared by Anglos and returned to service along the north bank of the Salt River was called Swilling Ditch, located near the present-day Sky Harbor Airport in Phoenix. Jack Swilling, organizer of the enterprise, was a pioneer, businessman, Confederate deserter, morphine addict, and drunk. Swilling is reported to have participated, together with prominent Arizona pioneer King S. Woosley, in the Massacre at Bloody Tanks—the slaughter of nineteen Apaches at a peace parley in 1864.

The Akimel O'odham (for many years called Pima Indians by outsiders) were the first suppliers of food to the Anglo outposts of the Salt River Valley area, sustaining them during their first decade of existence. In 1862 alone, the O'odham sold more than one million pounds of wheat to the U.S. Army and others, and thus enjoyed an unprecedented economic boom. By 1871 Swilling Ditch and other diversions were irrigating Anglo-controlled fields upstream from those of the O'odham, whose lands were left without access to river water and had to be abandoned. The O'odham found themselves with no reliable food source, nor access to the local agricultural market, when the Army at Camp McDowell switched to buying from Swilling and other pioneers.

Swilling's career trajectory of mercenary-turned-merchant was common among both Anglo and Mexican pioneers in the area, and characterizes many of the founders of the Salt River Project (SRP), whose genesis was the Swilling Ditch. As the oft-quoted adage goes, "He who controls the water controls the land." Today, thanks to over a century of giant federally-funded water projects such as the Roosevelt Dam and the Central Arizona Project, SRP is among the most powerful organizations in Arizona. SRP is still controlled by a veritable who's who of the Phoenix elite—just as it has been from the very beginning.

As the heart of a greater metro area known as "the Valley of the Sun," Phoenix is of course named after the bird of Egyptian mythology who immolates itself at the end of its life, and whose offspring rise from the ashes. The name was thought fitting for a city whose founders saw it as "rising from the ashes" of a "failed" Indian civilization—rising by using the very technology the Hohokam had themselves developed.

Sheridan, Thomas E. *Arizona*.

Jacoby, Karl. *Shadows at Dawn*.

The Salt River Project. *Taming of the Salt*. Phoenix. 1979.

PUERTO LIBERTAD · 81

The thermoelectric power plant at rural Puerto Libertad, Sonora, was built in the late 1970's and burns fuel brought in by tankers docked at its deep-water port. The electricity is sent into the decentralized international grid, but the plant burns at capacity during the long summer months when the millions of air conditioners in Hermosillo are running nonstop.

This poem was drafted in November 2011 during a teaching residency and cultural exchange at the high school in Puerto Libertad with international students visiting from the Verde Valley School.

SAGUARO FLATTENS DAVE GRINDMAN · 82

The story of the giant saguaro crushing its assailant is frequently retold and embellished in bars across Arizona; nonetheless it is rooted in a documented 1982 incident, the details of which are probably most thoroughly explored by Tom Miller.

Miller, Tom. *Jack Ruby's Kitchen Sink: Offbeat Travels Through America's Southwest.* (Washington: National Geographic Society, 2000).

SONORAN STRANGE: BARBWIRE · 83

This poem is set in Comala, Arizona. For more, read the story of the search for Pedro Páramo.

Rulfo, Juan. *Pedro Páramo.*
(Barcelona: Editorial Anagrama, 1953, 2004).

NAMING: TOMBSTONE · 85

See Sheridan's *Arizona* and Carter's *Boom, Bust, Boom* for more on the ephemeral boom-bust settlements of the Sonoran Strange Territory.

Carter, Bill. *Boom, Bust, Boom:*

Sheridan, Thomas E. *Arizona.*

ACKNOWLEDGEMENTS

Sonoran Strange is the fruit of seven years of labor, and as such there are innumerable people who came through my life during this time, so many of whom played roles in encouraging this book to happen.

The title of this book was born in the first email correspondence I ever had with mi hermano mago, the visualist Adam Cooper-Terán, as we were trying to articulate our shared experiences as culturally mixed young men born in the Sonoran Desert. Many of the seeds that later grew into the poems in this book were first sown in our conversations on long drives while on tour. The performance art version of *Sonoran Strange*—which we perform together—could only be what it is thanks to Adam's vision, expertise and dedication.

The collaboration and talent of Moisés Regla and Emmett White, compañeros de Verbo•bala, were key in the formation of this project and helping it survive through the tough times.

These poems owe a debt to Kristen Nelson, who sat with them for long hours, patiently helping them become what they were wanting to be. Jeanne Freeland's precise and caring eyes excised the orthographical demons and helped me see the work more clearly.

I'm grateful to Roberto Bedoya, Jeff Chang, and the organizer-participants of CultureStrike who provided a key venue for an early draft of this work, and gave me the energetic push to turn one long-form poem into a full-length book.

The development of the performance piece found support from Arizona Commission on the Arts, the Tucson Pima Arts Council and the Belle Foundation, who are all doing irreplaceable arts advocacy in a political climate that badly needs it. Bringing the performance to the world has benefited from the vision and sweat of Benjamin Hall Design, Carrie Morgan, Rhythm Industry Performance Factory, Flam Chen, Jay Ruby, Nemcatacoa Teatro, Mary Stephens, Casandra Hernandez, Mari Herreras, Luis Carrión, Andrea Zittlau, Carlos Contreras, Hakim Bellamy, Amanda Sutton, Lila Sánchez, Andrew Brown and Ray Vaughn Rai.

This book wouldn't have been possible to write anywhere but Tucson. Thanks to my community of artists and activists for first welcoming me when I moved back to Arizona from Mexico City in 2011, among them: Sarah Gonzales, Paco Velez, Maya Asher, Heather Grey, Daniela Ontiveros, Myrlin Hepworth, Enrique García, Amy Juan, Gabriel Sullivan, Vox Urbana, Rachel Bowditch, David Slutes, Casa Libre en la Solana, University of Arizona Poetry Center, Borderlands Theater, Arizona Between Nosotros, and the Tucson Poetry Festival.

I am thankful to my family for never doubting my poetic path, to my father for the gift of living history, and to Spring Winders for tolerating my long days at the desk and many nights away from home, working, learning and performing.

I want to acknowledge those whose names I am not fortunate enough to know, but whose lifetimes of hard work have given platform for these poems: storytellers, ancestors, teachers, rabble-rousers, farmers, activists, mothers. I'm thankful to the scholars and writers—whose many names shine in the notes—who have helped me put my understanding of my homeland in context, especially to Thomas Sheridan, Susana Rivera-Mills, Javier Trejo Sainz, Frederick Turner, Leslie Marmon Silko, Eduardo Galeano, Katherine Benton-Cohen, Eric Meeks and Lydia Otero.

Este libro va dedicado a todas las manos que han cultivado esta tierra, los corazones que la han sostenido, las caras mestizas y fronterizas que la han reflejado, y a los puños que aquí han reclamado la justicia. Eramos, somos y seremos orgullosamente *strange.*

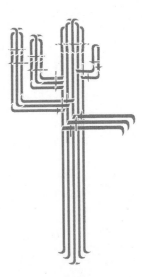